Behind the Veil

2004-2005 NMI
MISSION EDUCATION RESOURCES

✳ ✳ ✳

READING BOOKS

A DANGEROUS DEVOTION
Ordinary People in Extraordinary Adventures
by Carol Anne Eby

AFRICAN MOONS
by Juanita Moon

BEHIND THE VEIL
Taking Christ to Pakistanis
by Dallas Mucci

THE ROOKIE
Reflections of a New Missionary
by Tim Crutcher

TAKIN' IT TO THE STREETS
by Joe Colaizzi

WORDS OF LIFE AND LOVE
World Mission Literature Ministries
by Keith Schwanz

✳ ✳ ✳

ADULT MISSION EDUCATION RESOURCE BOOK

THE MISSION CALL
Edited by Wes Eby

DALLAS MUCCI

Behind the Veil

TAKING
CHRIST to
PAKISTANIS

Nazarene Publishing House
Kansas City, Missouri

Copyright 2004
by Nazarene Publishing House

ISBN 083-412-0801

Printed in the United States of America

Editor: Wes Eby
Cover Design: Darlene Filley

10   9   8   7   6   5   4   3   2   1

Contents

Dallas D. Mucci has served as superintendent of the Metro New York District, one of the largest districts in the Church of the Nazarene, since 1980. Prior to this time, he was a pastor in Chicago and Pittsburgh.

Both of Dr. Mucci's pastorates involved him in urban ministry. Now as superintendent in the Metro NYC area, the churches he serves speak English, Spanish, Korean, French Creole, Mandarin (China), Urdu (Pakistan), Hindi (India), and Japanese. Over 40 percent of the district is comprised of non-English-speaking congregations. During his tenure as superintendent, 70 new churches have been organized and church membership has nearly tripled to more than 12,000. In 1995 he led the mission to establish the Church of the Nazarene in Pakistan.

Dr. Mucci has earned degrees from Eastern Nazarene College (ENC) and the University of Chicago. He has taught at ENC as adjunct professor in the master's degree program in urban ministry.

Dr. Mucci has served the church in a variety of other ways, such as 15 years on the General Board, 5 years on the General Nazarene Youth International Council, chairman of the Board of Trustees of Eastern Nazarene College in Boston, and trustee of Nazarene Theological Seminary in Kansas City.

He is the author of *Weekday Nursery and Kindergarten Schools* and *This Pair of Hands: Dr. Howard Hamlin,* as well as numerous articles for various Christian and secular publishers.

Dallas Mucci is married to the former Sandra L. Hamlin, and they have four children: John, Dallas, Judy, and Bart.

Acknowledgments

I want to say thank you to

- Judy Mucci, my daughter, and Angela Oberdorfer, secretary of the Valley Stream Church of the Nazarene, for their tremendous help in typing the manuscript—several times.
- Rev. Alexander Robert, Violet Mall, and Aneel Mall, the Mall's son, in helping with the accuracy of facts and photographs.

Pakistan

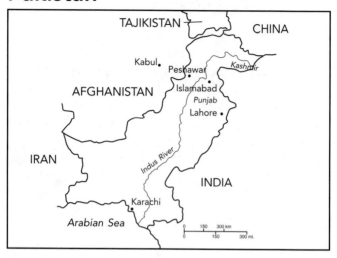

Libya

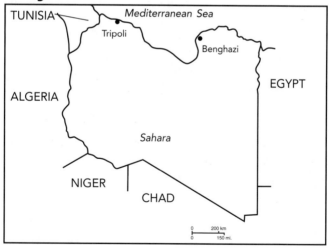

Introduction

"Christians Paying a Price for War" screamed the headline in *USA Today* in October 2002. The reporter wrote of a letter from a university delivered to a Christian hospital in Pakistan giving the recipient, Bushra Hadayat, some good news. She had successfully passed her final exams and, therefore, had earned a bachelor's degree in journalism. This 22-year-old woman had been working as a paramedic at the hospital to support her parents and younger siblings.

But Bushra never collected her hoped-for diploma. She, along with three other women, had been killed two months earlier when Islamic militants invaded the hospital property. The brutal attackers threw grenades at nurses, paramedics, and clerical workers, committing a violent act that shocked the community.

"The unthinkable is occurring with alarming regularity to Christians in Pakistan," Wiseman said. "Islamic extremists are targeting Pakistani Christians. In the past year almost 40 people have been killed in attacks on hospitals, churches, schools, and a charity office."*

The news of such horrific stories slowly filtered out of the country: . . . Five people, including two Americans, were killed when militants detonated grenades inside a church in Islamabad. . . . Six Pa-

---

*Paul Wiseman, "Christians Paying a Price for War," *USA Today*, October 4, 2002.

kistanis were shot dead when gunmen forced their way onto the grounds of a Christian school 40 miles north of Islamabad. . . . Extremists entered the office of a Christian charity in Karachi, gagged and bound eight workers, and shot each of them in the head.

Pakistan—the land *behind the veil*. While the veil has been the traditional dress for Pakistani women appearing in public, the *veil* is a symbol for all non-Muslims in a country where 97 percent of the population claim allegiance to the prophet Mohammed. Pakistani Christians have faced discrimination and threats. Blasphemy laws, which make it a crime punishable by death to defame Mohammed, have been used to terrorize Christians in business disputes and local rivalries. Until September 11, however, Pakistani Christians rarely had to fear for their lives. This has all changed since that infamous day in late summer of 2001.

> *The work of the Church of the Nazarene in Pakistan is God finding a good man—indeed, even two—who heard His call and responded.*

The Nazarene district superintendent in Pakistan, Rev. Alexander Robert, E-mailed New York in October 2002: "The government is concerned about the security of the churches. The local police cannot provide security guards, and they have asked us to provide them. We have two permanent arm licenses and must purchase two guns for the security guard at the David Mall Memorial Church. All of our churches face the same situation. We request that you continue praying for Nazarene churches in Pakistan."

Seven years earlier in the fall of 1995, Pastor David Mall and I stepped off the Pakistan International Airlines in Lahore, Pakistan, where we were met by our friend Alexander Robert. The World Mission Department in Kansas City had sent us to examine the prospects of officially opening mission work in the country.

Our wildest hopes would never have envisioned that by October 2002 there would be 23 organized churches and 7 new starts with a membership of 2,330. Even more impressive is that the Pakistanis in cooperation with Nazarene Compassionate Ministries International were assisting 6,000 Afghan families, providing primary schooling for 2,000 Afghan children, and setting up vocational training in Peshawar. So great has been the Nazarene influence that Yasim Kasib, president of the National Council in Afghanistan, has offered to give the Church of the Nazarene any one of three large houses to begin a Compassionate Ministries Center in Kabul.

God looked for a man to stand in the gap and make up the hedge. The work of the Church of the Nazarene in Pakistan is God finding a good man—indeed, even two—who heard His call and responded. This story, in large part, is how God prepared the men He would call to a needy land *behind the veil.*

1
Leaving Unexpectedly

"Doctor, doctor!" I hurried after the cardiologist in a Flushing, New York, hospital. "Doctor, you've just seen David Mall in the ICC unit, haven't you?"

As he turned to check on the person calling for his attention, he replied with a quizzical stare, "Yes?"

"What's his condition?" I pleaded. "Oh," I hurried to explain, "David is a pastor of our Flushing Indo-Pak Church of the Nazarene, and I'm Dallas Mucci, his district superintendent." I fumbled for credentials, but the doctor waved off my efforts with a reply that stunned me.

"His condition is grave. Massive heart attack. Until the full extent of the damage is known . . ." He stopped, and after a thoughtful pause continued, "My experience and preliminary tests prompt me to tell you that you should get his wife here. He is most critical."

As the doctor moved down the corridor, I was too numb to chase after him for any further explanation. I went back to ICCU, talked to one of David's children, and learned that they had not understood the full seriousness of the situation. Leaving

The congregation at Flushing Indo-Pak Church
of the Nazarene in New York

the hospital, I drove the six blocks to their home on
149th Street.

"Lord, surely You can heal this wonderful man,"
I prayed. "He's such a godly pastor and such a great
friend. If we lose him, too much is lost. Oh, God!
Forget that last bit. But I love this dear man. Please!"

The phone call informing me of David's hospi-
talization had called me away from the trip to High
Mountain Church of the Nazarene with my wife,
Sandy. We were going to prepare for our annual
Metro New York pastor and spouses' Christmas luncheon. I had sent her on to New Jersey, and I drove
to Flushing. I dialed her on my cell phone.

"David had a terrible heart attack!" I said without a preface. "The doctor has convinced me that
the situation is beyond usual medical control. Please

pray, and urge the people helping you to pray. And I'll try to update you." I hurriedly finished. "I've come to take Violet to the hospital, She doesn't understand yet how bad David is."

Turning off the cell phone, I struggled to understand the reality. *How can I tell Violet?* I wondered as I parked the car in front of the Mall residence. Just a few weeks before, David and I had discussed our next trip to Pakistan.

Violet acted as if she were surprised to see me. She greeted me and then rather matter-of-factly told me that David had taken ill and was in the hospital. Though a nurse, she was not aware of the seriousness of the heart

> *Walking back into the ICCU, I noted with new hope that all of the vital signs had improved.*

attack. First, I led in fervent prayer for the doctor and God's intervention. Then I asked her to sit.

Violet wept as I told her of my talk with the physician. "Your husband's heart attack was massive," I said, trying to be gentle yet conveying the gravity of his condition. She quickly made necessary preparations, and we were on our way.

Walking back into the ICCU, I noted with new hope that all of the vital signs had improved. In fact, the two most important showed marked improvement within the last couple of hours. *Could it be? . . . It could be!* I wildly hoped.

The doctor had returned to check on David, and he seemed pleased by the vital signs. Before we could ask him, he called us aside and quietly, emotionlessly explained, "Rev. Mall's heart is severely damaged, and there is little hope for any good recovery—short of a miracle." Then he was gone.

We all prayed. Vital signs did not drop with the doctor's report to us.

Then David opened his eyes and spoke to me. It was vintage David. "How is Sister Mucci . . . and your family? . . . Thanks for being here, . . . but you are so busy?"

"Oh, she is well." I fought to hold back the tears.

Remembering the pastors and spouses' luncheon, David said that he doubted he would be able to make it. I assured him that we would miss him. Then he said, "I have much pain at times." Smiling, he lapsed back into sleep.

I paced the corridor as other family members and Violet remained with David, hoping against hope that God was intervening. The vital signs stayed up, but David remained quiet and asleep under sedation. The family urged me to go and help Sandy finish preparing for the luncheon with the assurance I could return in the evening for another visit.

While driving up Harlem River Drive to the George Washington Bridge entrance, praying and meditating, I resolved to return to the hospital. A call to Sandy brought her full agreement that I should abort the trip and be with the Mall family.

Speeding along I hoped for another opportunity to talk with my dear friend. *Wouldn't it be a glorious divine intervention for God to raise him up?* I thought.

I'd have a great Christmas message for tomorrow's luncheon: God healed that heart! "You are able, Lord," I began singing as I drove into Flushing.

Turning the corner of the hallway that led to ICCU, I was met by the entire family. "Daddy is gone." Tears flowed. Grief, even shock, weighed

Rev. Elvis Naqui and Mrs. Violet Mall, pastors of Flushing Indo-Pak Church after Rev. Mall's death

heavy on each one. Then Violet added, "He is with Jesus."

How could I comfort them? I sought for help. "Oh, God, we have no Pakistani like David in the Church of the Nazarene," I prayed silently. We all needed the God of all comfort.

Later, alone in my car, I wept. He was too young, too valuable to our Pakistani ministry. This is no way to finish.

2
Achieving Success

Five-and-a-half-year-old David walked the five miles to school, remembering a different time. A time when there was enough and the food was good. A time when his illiterate father joyfully celebrated the new harvest on the land given him in India. A time when religious ideas were not such a threat. David remembered a better time.

All had changed—those good, happy times of plenty—with the partition of India's northern Punjab into the country of Pakistan. The Muslims had taken control of the government, and David, his parents, and five siblings were quickly expelled from their productive farm. They moved into a squalid village with no school. David even remembered that his enraged and helpless father talked about a fine assessed to him before they were evicted.

Little David was hungry most of the time. But he was most interested in learning, and the long walks were made easier because he continued to learn new things. Then in sixth grade, he learned English, his fourth language. He already spoke Urdu, Tamil, and Hindi, languages common to the Punjab and Pakistan.

The English language opened up a whole new world to this famished son of a now desperate day laborer trying to feed his large family. David read English newspapers and learned of another way of life. In his seventh year of schooling, his grades were outstanding, for he absorbed any bit of English literature and writing he could find. All that seemed to end, however, during this year. His parents, to his regret, found him a job in a bicycle repair shop.

Four weeks into the job, a teacher from a nearby village school came and convinced David's parents that he should return and finish school. "This was the real beginning of the full life that God was preparing me for," David joyfully recounted on our trip to officially open Nazarene work in Pakistan in 1995.

As David prepared for high school, again a concerned, unnamed teacher intervened and provided much needed assistance. Graduating in May 1959, David had exceeded the grandest hopes of himself or his family—a high school diploma. But even this milestone was not enough to secure a desired position.

David visited a friend in the larger town of Mouton, a day's journey, where he found a demanding canal-digging job. He became quite proud of his callused hands. The only affordable lodging was a room with a pastor. Although David was not a Christian, he had learned to seize every opportunity to survive and learn.

His callused hands were hardened just enough to be comfortable when a former teacher encountered David in the pastor's home. The instructor, quite surprised to find David there, promptly urged him to enroll in college.

What a wonderful but impossible dream! David thought, smiling to himself.

The former mentor touched the hopes of this determined young man. "You must try, David. What can you lose?" The teacher's final promise "God can help you," however, was lost on an unbelieving David. But over time, that promise proved to be true.

Packing his total goods in a knapsack, David headed back to his village. His mother was happy but puzzled by his unexpected return. She was even more surprised upon learning her son was going to try for college. She gave her blessing.

David found a pastor in the community where he finished high school who arranged with the village headman to write a letter on his behalf. Almost immediately the answer came back: David's admission to the Methodist College in the great city of Lahore had been approved. The calluses were nearly gone by his departure in July 1960. His very first train ride was the trip to Lahore and college.

This one-time peasant boy, now a man, accomplished what no one from his depressed little village had ever done.

Later, he learned that the Methodist College was highly regarded with its largely American-born and -trained faculty. He was considered such a good prospective stu-

David Mall

dent that the Methodist missionaries granted him a work-study scholarship for the three-year course.

But college proved to be more difficult than David had anticipated. He studied and worked hard in his first year. His reward was earning above average marks in all his classes. His spiritual life, however, never developed. Instead he picked up new vices, including cigarettes.

David's second year was different, as he flunked two subjects, largely the result of his newly acquired lifestyle. The college gave him a second chance during summer school, and the young man controlled himself enough to pass the failed courses. Doggedly he fought through the third year and graduated.

In 1965 David enrolled in Pakistan Government College in Mouton and earned a bachelor's degree in education, granted the following May. The influence of caring teachers had helped him choose and then persevere to prepare for a teaching career. This one-time peasant boy, now a man, accomplished what no one from his depressed little village had ever done.

A new and demanding life had just begun for Mr. David Mall. In June 1966, he moved to Karachi, Pakistan's greatest city, to teach in a small school.

Unexpectedly, he received a letter from his parents, informing him it was time to marry, and they had chosen a bride. David learned his wife-to-be was a nurse, but he knew little of her, especially her abiding Christian faith. Dutifully David was married to Violet Sunderdass on December 28, 1966, in his tiny hometown. Within days of the wedding, he was back in Karachi, and Violet returned to the hospital in Lahore where she was employed.

But David found this separation unacceptable. Eight months later he landed a job teaching English at the Roman Catholic high school in Lahore and was finally reunited with Violet. He rose quickly in the Catholic school system, teaching in two different high schools. Three years later he was appointed second headmaster.

David and Violet, teacher and nurse, both advancing in their professions, looked proudly at the home they had purchased in Lahore. Soon they brought their aging parents to live with them. "It was the best thing I could do." David's eyes sparkled as he remembered this great event in his life. And the good life continued with the birth of Rebecca on July 13, 1969, named by her mother.

To David and his family, he had achieved success. Indeed, he was Mr. Success!

3
Encountering Christ

Three months before Violet became the arranged bride for David, she had a dramatic encounter with Jesus Christ. Two Christian nurses, Dean and Gulo, coworkers in the hospital, had been witnessing to her. On one occasion they had taken her to a house prayer meeting where the Holy Spirit convicted her. "I was powerfully moved," Violet says, "but did not yield."

September 27 was her day off. Suffering from a severe headache, Violet went to Dean and Gulo's room. When she arrived, both were praying. Touched by the Spirit, Violet quickly knelt down, crying out to God. "What must I do? O my God, what must I do?" she prayed. "O my God, save me!"

More than three decades later, Violet shouts as she remembers that night. "I promised God that I would spend my whole life for His glorification, and I would give Him all my perplexities and worries. With that prayer I saw in my mind's eye a mountain, and on a very bright road my Jesus was coming toward me. And I was flying to heaven. All my worries were gone. I was going to my Redeemer who was crucified for my sin."

The weeks following her conversion were splendid for Violet. "The richness of the Holy Spirit assisted me in living the life as a true Christian," she says. "I began enjoying the glorious new fellowship with God's people. I kept myself busy with prayer and the breaking of bread."

When Violet married David Mall, she realized he was a worldly man. He insisted that her sharing about God with other people be reduced. "My spiritual condition went from bad to worse," she says. "But I prayed fervently, 'O my Savior, when will You bring change in the life of my husband?'"

So in the midst of happy circumstances and successes—a baby daughter, a new home, rewarding careers—Violet was struggling in her marriage, her spiritual life nearly shattered.

A few weeks later after another difficult day, she had a dream. "I came back from hospital duty," she recalls, "and I saw a lion standing at my door that said, 'Don't worry. I'm the guardian of your house.' I was dumbfounded to hear the lion speak."

This dream haunted her. When she shared it with her friends Dean and Gulo, at first they hesitated. Then both nurses spoke at the same time and with the same message.

"In Revelation the lion is Jesus himself," they told her. "He is your Guardian. Therefore, do not worry, and don't tell David either. Only pray. He, the Lion Christ, will appoint some preacher on His appointed time to give testimony."

This interpretation of her dream filled her with assurance. "It brought a profound peace to my heart," Violet says. "But I prayed for several years before that testimony came."

Much was changing in the Muslim world in 1970 with God using the evil efforts of people to bring salvation to many. Muammar Khaddafi gained control of the government in Libya and installed a limited Muslim state. At the same time he nationalized all the oil fields, basically securing profits that previously had gone to American oil companies. With this grasp of American assets, Libya would grow into the richest country per capita income on the African continent. However, the nationalization of the oil industry caused the flight of the much-needed American technicians. Libya was about to flounder.

Khaddafi turned to the Middle East and Pakistan, enticing technically skilled people with much higher wages. His recruiters combed Pakistan. In addition to oil field expertise, there was a need for health professionals and teachers—specifically English teachers.

Complicating everything for David and Violet was the election of Z. A. Bhutto as Pakistan's prime minister. Under his leadership came the radical introduction of Islamic socialism. In implementing his educational policies, the government took over and nationalized all private Urdu medium schools. Also, the process of converting from Islam to the Christian faith would soon become a capital crime.

In this political and social environment, it was easy for Violet to accept an offer of a high-paying nursing job in Libya. In April 1972 Violet moved by herself to this north African nation. Although this relieved some of the tensions at home, her real peace was the promise that God would send a preacher to give testimony to David. She continued to pray each day with that assurance.

The situation for non-Muslims continued to deteriorate in Pakistan. The Catholic schools were either kicked out or accepted nationalization. Most schools took the latter route. War with India seemed imminent, and this inflicted a wave of terror on the small Christian population in Lahore. When war came, persecution increased. Fortunately, Violet was in Libya. Though she did manage a trip to Lahore in December 1972 in spite of the war, she had to make a fast return to Libya the next month.

We can get rich in Libya, David thought, and at the right time, we can return to Lahore. Then I can set ourselves up quite handsomely.

David, angry and frustrated, contemplated leaving Lahore and his beloved home. The dramatic change in the schools made it almost impossible to teach, and wages declined. The war brought even greater poverty to the country.

In desperation, David finally decided to join fellow Pakistanis in Libya. Securing a visa easily, he departed Pakistan with his child in January of 1973.

The dreams of wealth returned as David considered the wages for both him and his wife. *We can get rich in Libya*, David thought, *and at the right time, we can return to Lahore. Then I can set ourselves up quite handsomely.*

Violet had been shocked to learn upon her arrival in Libya that Khaddafi had turned most of the former Christian churches into offices. Officially, there was suppose to be religious freedom, but Christian groups were harassed and lost their church properties. The spiritual drought in Libya was severe. Violet could not find a single church in Tripoli—not even a small group. When David decided to join his wife, she thought, *How can God's promise to me be kept? I don't even have a church to attend.*

At the very time David was en route to Libya, his wife had another dream. "Violet, the dark clouds from your house have gone away," a voice said. "All the dark clothes of David have been washed in the water tank in the middle of the garden." Having no idea how this could happen, she trusted God. Her fears were dispelled by the simple faith that God would fulfill the promise. But her husband came, unchanged and unwashed.

David continued his bad habits and vices in Libya, and life was as difficult for the couple as it had been in Lahore. A neighbor, who obviously knew Violet was a Christian, wondered out loud to the Malls if David might start a church. "I'm in Libya to make money!" David said to the neighbor, scoffing at such a preposterous idea. God's work didn't have any place in David's plans.

A couple of weeks later, evangelist Bashir Almas

David and Violet Mall in Libya

—"sent by God," David claimed—came to preach for 15 days in Benghazi, Libya's new capital city. Violet was elated to learn of this unexpected break in the spiritual drought. *Could this be the testimony to David that God has promised?* she wondered. Violet was in the first service led by the fiery preacher Almas. David, instead, went to a movie. Later, some friends of Violet managed to get David in one service. But his only response was that he didn't like the speaking style of the evangelist.

Near the end of the revival, the Malls planned their usual routine: Violet would go to church and David would go to a movie. He left with a friend for the theater, when, as David put it, "God struck me! It was the Holy Spirit who convicted me to go to church." He left his friend at the theater door and returned home to accompany his wife to the revival meeting.

Violet was both shocked and excited when David announced his intentions. He picked up Violet's Bible—which he had never read—tucked it under his arm, and escorted her down the street.

During the service, he tried to sing the songs, but not with much success. He listened intently to the sermon from Revelation 3:14-22 and could not escape its penetrating message. Although he did not go forward at the invitation, David repented and sought God's forgiveness in a private prayer of confession. The love of wealth evaporated as he silently prayed. God's deliverance of his evil habits was supplemented by an abiding hunger to know Christ through the revealed Scripture.

David Mall was baptized in the Mediterranean Sea on April 2, 1975, confirming that he was truly a new person. Some of the witnesses were surprised and laughed in jest. But Violet rejoiced and cried, reveling in God's answer to her prayer.

When David's friends came to take him to the theater, he refused to go with them. "No more movies and vices—even the cigarettes are gone," David testified to his startled buddies. "The study of God's Word, the Bible, has become the joy of my life." The men, astonished and jolted by David's declaration, left quickly.

4

Starting in Ministry

"You'll soon be deported," a Muslim scorner warned David. "Then what will you do?"

"We have to do what we're doing," David replied. "This is God's will and work for us. We cannot stop, even if many threats come."

The Malls continued to witness, unfazed and unafraid.

After David's sudden conversion, he and Violet entered an extended time of fasting and prayer, seeking God's direction and prescription for keeping their faith warm and bright. Then the Spirit moved. Changes came in rapid succession, beginning with a total surprise.

"I knew," David said, "that God's Spirit would lead us. I just knew it, and I knew it would be right." The words of evangelist Almas kept alive the search for spiritual certitude, but David was unprepared for the great preface to that revelation.

"I was overawed," he said, "by the powerful and abiding sense of God's great love for us." This pervading love energized David and purified his heart by faith. The experience of God's unconditional love became a source of strength for David throughout his entire life.

The substance of God's revelation to both David and Violet following their fast came so clearly. "You are now My witnesses," they heard the Lord say. They opened the Bible and learned what that meant.

But what will we say in our witness? they wondered. They turned to prayer, and this was their petition: "O God, if You want us to serve You, give us the word. We don't know how to serve You."

The Lord then directed them to Psalm 2, and they settled on this as the first message they would share with others. "We just started going house-to-house, preaching the Word of God," Violet says. The courageous couple didn't consider any consequence that might come from preaching to Muslims. For the Malls, it was a simple, compelling joy of witnessing to everyone. That is why they could boldly say to their Muslim scoffer, "We have to do what we're doing."

The joy of witnessing for David was epitomized in the airport in Delhi, India. He and I were waiting for our flight to Lahore in 1995. A young man sat down next to us. David quickly introduced us and engaged the stranger in conversation. We learned he was a Pakistani by birth but a naturalized citizen of Scotland, working in Glasgow. This young engineer was returning to his adopted homeland from a visit to his family in Pakistan.

"We are Christians," David told him. The man squirmed a bit, but David continued in his warm, engaging way. The conversation turned philosophical, and we all shared our views. But David drew the discussion back to the central hope in Christ. Though the young man did not make a commitment to the Lord, David gathered all the particulars so a Nazarene church in Glasgow might continue to witness. We both prayed for this engineer, David fully confident that God would take it from there.

After work and on days off, David and Violet, Bible in hand, undaunted by scorn from David's former friends, went house-to-house, preaching and teaching. Soon their ministry expanded into the streets of Benghazi. Even though the mocking increased, the Malls persevered. And in course of witnessing they met a kindred spirit in Mr. Benjamin John, who joined forces with them.

New challenges to the fledgling ministry came through the Mall family. Little Rebecca was forbidden to play with other children when ugly blisters appeared on her face. Rebecca's ostracism was painfully frightening to them. The applied medicines were of questionable benefit. "What will happen if her face doesn't heal?" her concerned parents fretted. They read the Bible. The house-to-house visits were nearly stopped by the alarming illness.

The happy parents saw that Rebecca was well. Her blisters were gone; the wounds, healed.

Violet raised the question, "Why shouldn't we go to the Doctor of doctors who has the power to even raise the dead?" They did. The

Malls carefully followed the biblical instruction of anointing with oil and offering one single prayer, "Father, please heal our daughter."

"At about four A.M.," Violet says, "a voice seemed to say, 'Violet, get up. I have healed your daughter.' I arose and asked David to turn on the light." The happy parents saw that Rebecca was well. Her blisters were gone; the wounds, healed. In a few days her face was unmarked. Their hearts abounded in joy and gratitude to God.

Another crisis that nearly shook their faith came six days later when their son Nayyar became ill quite suddenly. His body was covered with blisters. The boy writhed in pain. Violet, the nurse, thought he had been bitten by a snake. His condition worsened. Could they believe that God would answer them with another healing? God had healed Rebecca completely.

The Malls read the Bible and prayed. Once again they applied the anointing oil, asking God to touch their boy and heal him of this unknown disease. No voice. No visit. Then two days later, Nayyar was suddenly and completely well. The celebration of praise was explosive, extolling the faithfulness of God.

"This healing confirmed for us the power of God and the Holy Spirit's call on our lives," David said. With new joy and resolve the Malls resumed their door-to-door preaching. "It was crystal clear," David said, "that God had called us to a special lifetime of service. We had the full assurance again of the Holy Spirit within us."

Being confident of God's call, David went to their one-time neighbor who had suggested, upon his arrival in Libya, that he start a church. David was surprised to learn the man didn't even have a Bible. Yet in their visit, the two men agreed on a plan and prepared to begin services.

The Malls, Benjamin John, and the homeowner started a house church in Benghazi, saturating this venture in prayer. David and Violet took their three children—Rebecca, Nayyar, and Aneel—with them out in the street to preach and invite people to church. The verbal abuse encountered didn't stop or set back this minister. David was all the more determined.

But the Malls faith was tested again. Even though their joy of dramatic healings was fresh, they had secured a place for a house church, and they had two brothers to assist them, the work did not flourish. For six months they went house-to-house and preaching on many streets, still no one seemed moved by the Holy Spirit.

"We were hopeful at first; then we worried," Violet says. "We prayed and nothing happened as a result of our efforts. But we continued to pray and preach and visit." She remembers one particular prayer: "O God, change the hearts of the people and let them experience yourself. Let us move forward, and through us may Your name be glorified and praised." But no one responded in faith.

One night Violet had another puzzling dream. In the prayer room of their apartment, many flower-pots were spread around haphazardly, and she saw herself neatly arranging them. She told no one of the dream. Then a man, who was a back-slider, returned to Christ and joined with them. When she told him about the dream, he said, "The flowerpots are peo-ple God will redeem as a re-sult of your faithful service."

> *Violet remembered how God encouraged her by the flowerpot dream.*

Time marched on. Still no victories.

One month later and seven months after the start of the house church, one couple accepted Christ. Amid the rejoicing and praises to God, Violet remembered how God encouraged her by the flow-erpot dream. The next week a lady was saved. With-in two months another couple was converted, and growth continued. The numbers increased, and the house church became a true center of holy light. God had taken an English teacher and a nurse, trans-formed them by His grace, and sent them out. The Holy Spirit became their teacher as they began to preach and teach a holy life.

As this growing congregation sang lustily and prayed fervently, the Muslim family that shared their townhouse began to object. While David pleaded with his "disturbed" neighbors, his entreaty only led to a visit from the Libyan police, who ordered David to cease leading Christian services—*immediately.* In addition the police insisted that the Malls completely move out of the neighborhood. The church was closed. Just like that.

The small Christian group began to search for a

new place. Every good lead turned to a disappointment. No location could be found in all of Benghazi. No support from any church of other Christians was available or forthcoming.

Stubbornly, this small band of Jesus' followers believed that God was building a church. *But where?* they wondered. They had no prospective place to worship. Would the church live or die?

5

Facing Challenges

"Would you help us move?" the stranger asked David.

David Mall was sitting in a public area in May 1976 when he was approached by a Muslim man with three children.

"My boss is going to Germany," the man explained, "and I have bought his house. But I need some help. Can you?"

David agreed. As he assisted with the move, he discovered the rented house the Muslim was leaving might be available. David immediately requested the stranger's assistance in obtaining a new home, and the grateful man obliged by renting the large apartment he was vacating to the Malls.

"This was a witness to our people," David said. The church services were held in the living room; people sat on the carpet. One of their three bedrooms became a Sunday School room. Indeed, a wonderful new beginning!

Three weeks later, a furious Libyan who lived on the sixth floor confronted David. "Don't play your music and worship in your apartment! Stop it now, or . . . !"

Apparently the Malls would be evicted again.

A neighbor woman who witnessed the angry threats against David and his group of Christians was offended. "Don't be afraid," she quietly told Violet. "I'll help you."

When a military policeman came to their apartment, David's hopes were dashed. But he was wrong. It was the policeman's wife who had defended the Christians and convinced her husband to protect them. He only wanted David to keep the services as quiet as possible. The police officer then visited the angry neighbor and suggested that if he didn't like the area he could move out. For the next five years, this house church received police protection.

At the time of David's conversion, he had met a well-educated Pakistani, Alexander Robert. Mr. Robert had attended services with a Christian group meeting in a Catholic church. His background was primarily Anglican with Catholic primary school training.

"David Mall and Benjamin John often visited my wife, Susan, and me," says Alexander. "We enjoyed these cheerful men, and their visits prompted us to attend their house church called Convocation of Believers."

Alexander remembers great debates with his friends, David and Benjamin, over the matters of Christian faith. "I was, at best, a nominal Christian, so I didn't agree with adult baptism and several other areas of doctrine. But the preaching on repentance and regeneration stirred me. Brother Benjamin was not very literate, but his bold and enthusiastic proclamation of God's Word forced me to think. I had great pride in my worldly knowledge compared with this servant of God.

"One night," Alexander confesses, "the light of faith kindled in my heart. I wept bitterly over my proud sinful nature. I cried out, 'Lord Jesus, I'm a sinner. I need Your forgiveness.' My pride had kept me from yielding before this moment. Then the peace of God came into my heart."

Pastor David Mall and Benjamin John baptized Alexander Robert in the Mediterranean Sea on November 18, 1977. One month later, Alexander's wife, Susan, gave her life to Christ, and she was baptized too.

The Benghazi congregation rejoicing after a baptism in the Mediterranean Sea. David Mall on far left; Alexander Robert in center with sunglasses.

The house church in Benghazi continued to grow as many new families accepted Christ until 60 people filled the Mall's apartment. And as Alexander stepped into his exciting new life, David guided him to ask the Lord to reveal the gifts and talents he [Alexander] had for service. The revelation came quickly. Alexander began to interpret sermons into Urdu, English, and Arabic languages. Since David didn't drive, Alexander drove his pastor to various homes for visits and prayer. And as other talents became obvious, the church developed more and more.

God's hand continued to write the script, which He had started years before, for the Church of the Nazarene to begin work in the Muslim nation of Pakistan. Alexander Robert would become God's human instrument.

Mr. Robert had completed a master's degree in the College of Education in Lahore and secured an excellent teaching post at Model High School. The Muslim takeover in 1972, however, forced him to seek employment and opportunity in another country. His elderly mother suggested that he go to Libya, earn enough money, and move to the United States. Shortly after, his sister, Rita Noor, who was nursing in Libya, invited him to check out the job situation in the north Africa country. He moved there in October 1974.

"I thank the Lord," Alexander says, "that during the next 10 years He prepared me for the opening of the church in Pakistan. My career provided good

The Benghazi congregation in worship. David Mall on far right; Alexander Robert holding child.

wages, but the varied nature of my life there was *per-fect* preparation. I learned to drive. I learned Arabic. I learned international commercial knowledge and office administration. I learned telex and computers. All these blessings, provided by Muslim Libya, were added to my teacher training and skills."

Mr. Robert became the executive director of the small but vigorous house church in Benghazi. Much like what David experienced, Alexander wrote to a friend, "Worldly trends are gone from my life. I am experiencing a strange but wonderful change in my lifestyle. Now the study of the Bible is No. 1 in my life."

In 1977 a Pakistani family that had been brought to the Lord through David's ministry accepted a job opportunity in Tulsa, Oklahoma. In their search for a church, they found the Church of the Nazarene and joined it. They believed the biblical teaching was similar to the Convocation of Believers in Libya. They surprised David with the challenge to go to America and fully prepare himself for ministry, suggesting, of course, Nazarene Theological Seminary (NTS) in Kansas City.

Bewildered, depressed, and alone in an Italian hotel, David broke down and cried.

At first David rejected the idea. But as he prayed, he was swayed to consider the suggestion, since Jesus' disciples had three years of training before ministry. He called it "a new revelation."

The next year he applied for a visa from Libya to study in the United States, but permission was denied. In the next several months, he made several unsuccessful attempts to move to Kansas City but failed each time. In one effort made through Italy, he missed the key contact person by two hours. Bewildered, depressed, and alone in an Italian hotel, David broke down and cried. In the midst of his agony, the Lord whispered, "Trust Me, David. I'm going to help you." That lifted his spirit, giving him new hope. David returned to Libya to pastor while continuing his efforts to attend seminary.

Everything came together in 1980—the letter of acceptance from NTS and a visa for passage. In early September David caught the plane for London, leaving his family in Benghazi because he had no permission for his family to travel with him.

In the meantime, the Libyan police had begun to investigate all Christian ministers. Most pastors were mistreated severely and placed under close scrutiny. David had left just two days before the police came looking for him.

A driver picked up David at the Kansas City airport and took him to NTS, where he received one weeks' lodging at King Conference Center. Next, he had to find a place to live.

Rev. Mall had placed Alexander Robert as leader in personal evangelism and church administration. While David studied at NTS, he nurtured the small church in Libya with encouraging letters and phone chats. He sent Alexander the Articles of Faith of the Church of the Nazarene. "The articles gave me a new dimension," Alexander says, "and opened the holiness doctrine to me."

6

Tackling Seminary

A monumental challenge! This is the only way to describe David's first year at Nazarene Theological Seminary. He was asked to leave the apartment NTS had located, because the managers considered him a Black man.

Even more difficult was the refusal of the government to allow his family to join him. Violet and the children had returned to Pakistan to live and work, anticipating a quick approval to join their husband and father in the States. Instead, they were stuck in Pakistan. Every effort to get to Kansas City failed!

In the midst of David's loneliness, God gifted him with a wonderful substitute family at the Nall Avenue Church of the Nazarene in Prairie Village, Kansas. There he met Dean Quillin and Bob Soulia. "These brothers prayed for me," David said. "Then Dean and his wife took me to their home for dinner. From that meal and encounter came a great Christian brother. In fact, Nall Avenue is the greatest church, for they loved me. They literally were God's instrument that made it possible for me to graduate from the Seminary. They are loving, caring Nazarenes."

A whole year passed with no progress on visas for David's family. Doubts flooded in. He shared this disheartening situation with his friend Dean, who covenanted to pray with him. David was so discouraged that he wondered if he had missed God's direction. He resolved that he would return to Libya if the family did not come before September.

Then without any advanced notice, permission was granted in June 1981. A happy reunion took place at the Kansas City airport. David would stay and graduate.

This new joy, however, generated a new set of challenges. David's visa only allowed him to obtain part-time work at the seminary, hardly sufficient to pay tuition and provide food, clothing, and housing for a family of five. As Christmas neared that year, the Malls were destitute.

David's studies were difficult; his job exhausted him. Adding to this was the grim reality of hunger. Perhaps his studies would have to end with this next semester, he often wondered. So the seminarian prayed in desperation. The answer came, "Didn't I tell you to depend upon Me? Now do it." Doggedly David continued in school and on the job.

Some new Nazarene friends had given the Malls a car, but on one particular Sunday, there was no gasoline. They missed church. When Dean checked on David, he extracted the truth of the Malls' financial situation. Christmas that year became more than survival for

Other miracles —and they were miracles— overwhelmed us.

this Pakistani family in a strange country, because the Nall Avenue church met their needs.

"Other miracles—and they *were* miracles—overwhelmed us, for we did not know the persons who sent food and paid the apartment rent until I graduated," David remembered with thanksgiving. Plus, his friends in Tulsa even paid his seminary tuition.

Violet was then able to study English. This language training provided her the skills to take the United States exams to validate her nursing credentials. The Malls received the gift of another car, so Violet could continue her studies and secure part-time work.

David and Violet Mall with their children *(l. to r.)* Nayyar, Rebecca, and Aneel, 1983

David had not lost contact with the Convocation of Believers in Libya. He continued to educate Alexander Robert on the biblical doctrines of the Church of the Nazarene. As the job situation slowed in Libya, the government began to withdraw the visas of foreign nationals. The church began to shrink. Then Alexander and his family were sent back to Pakistan. David called and wrote to the "little church" in Libya. And they have kept the faith to this date, even though Pastor Alexander had to return to Lahore.

David graduated from NTS in May 1985. Since he could not return to Libya, he sought the Lord for the future. "Where do You want me to go?" he asked.

He traveled down to Tulsa where his friends were living, but no door for ministry opened there. L. Guy Nees, then director of World Mission, called David and talked to him about Pakistan. However, visa problems blocked the possibility of starting new work in that country. He was instructed to send résumés to district superintendents in America, but nothing came of that effort.

Rev. Phil Patalano, an NTS student from Connecticut, called me, since I was his district superintendent, and urged me to talk with David Mall about New York. Phil had already done demographic studies and knew that New York City had the largest Pakistani enclave in the States.

"Many Pakistani people want to go to New York," David wrote me. "And when I came to Kansas City, I had the same hope of going there. But after three and a half years of the American press disparaging New York, I had lost interest in this large city."

But in late winter of 1986, David and Violet informed me that God had indeed called them to New York, and they would move to Flushing where the largest number of Pakistanis lived. Pastor Barry Whetstone and the members of Flushing First Church opened their homes and treasury to the Malls. The work was underway.

Flushing First Nazarenes cared, mentored, and assisted in the difficult adjustments for this new Pakistani minister and family. The members provided housing and a church in the early years of establishing Flushing Indo-Pak Church of the Nazarene.

David, a bivocational church planter in the Big Apple, also kept up his contact in Libya and his mentoring of Alexander Robert in Pakistan.

I answered my telephone one day in June 1992 and heard the excited voice of my friend and pastor, David Mall. "Alexander Robert is here and wants to meet you. We'll come any time."

"Who is Alexander Robert?" I asked.

"I guess you've forgotten a conversation of years ago when I first came here. He is a Pakistani friend, and he led the church in Libya after I left. When can we get together?"

7

Laying the Foundation

Sandy and I were introduced to the Alexander Robert family a few days later at lunch in a Queens restaurant. After some small talk, David raised the possibility of starting the Church of the Nazarene in Pakistan. I listened carefully as these two friends discussed and planned for starting a holiness ministry in this Muslim country.

The Roberts visited other people in the United States. Upon their return to New York, their interest in planting the church in Pakistan had expanded. We talked again about how this could happen. As a result, Alexander asked if I would interact with the World Mission Department about this matter. Even though I agreed, I remained tentative, wondering.

Before the Roberts returned to Pakistan, we introduced them to the Metro New York District family at Camp Taconic in August. Alexander and his family dedicated their lives to beginning a mission, and New York Nazarenes pledged to pray for God's direction in establishing the work. The Roberts returned to the land of their birth, and life hurried on in New York.

At the General Board meeting in 1993, I talked with Steve Weber, who was involved in new fields' work in World Mission at that time, and Louie Bustle, World Mission director, about my visit with Alexander and the prospect of work in Pakistan. Both church leaders were interested. They told me to keep in contact with Alexander and report back to them.

Unknown to me, Pastor Mall received the Robert family into the membership of Flushing Indo-Pak Church and sent them back to Pakistan to begin Nazarene work. And they did just that.

Alexander was already being prepared for such an assignment a decade earlier in 1984. "The teaching profession and experience gained," he says, "aroused my interest and zeal to start my own educational program." He had looked at the office building of Rendel, Palmer, and Tritton and dreamed of a school building of such dimensions. "While working there I visualized a school program in Pakistan some day."

When the Roberts returned to Pakistan from Libya, they had saved enough money to start a primary school in Lahore. "Greater than the money was the new joy of salvation and peace of heart found in Libya," he wrote to David. "I was a different person and had come to rely on God more than anything else."

In 1984 Alexander purchased a building that became the St. Maria School. On opening day, 25 children enrolled, and by the end of the first year the number reached 100. Susan Robert, Alexander's wife, was the dean of girls and assisted in school administration. Two years later Alexander erected a small administration building and constructed four more classrooms the following year. As the enrollment increased, he added a second floor. By 1991 there were 300 students. The Roberts were so committed to this ministry that they sold their small house to acquire the capital to add a third floor and build a small apartment.

Primary in the curriculum were Bible study and evangelism, since most children came from name-only Christian or nonreligious backgrounds. "The nine teachers, Susan, and myself were determined to teach the students about a life that would honor almighty God and thus bless all people," Alexander explains passionately.

Today this 20-room school with a staff of 13 teachers and 2 helpers serves 375 students in the midst of a sub-poverty area with open sewers in the center of the streets. The children's parents are largely preliterate, and this had trapped them in debilitating poverty. In this pain and dire need many have turned to all kinds of vices.

> *The excellence of the school attracted Muslim students until they comprised 20 percent of the enrollment.*

The excellence of the school attracted Muslim students until they comprised 20 percent of the enrollment. While the Muslim parents were able to afford the fees, many of the impoverished people could not pay. Even with mea-

A Nazarene school in Lahore, Pakistan

ger resources, the school was able to meet all the government regulations and thereby receive full recognition.

Alexander requested a visa from the U.S. Embassy in 1987, which was granted. With the school well established, he took his family to visit his spiritual mentor, David Mall, in New York. By this time, David had already helped organize the Flushing Indo-Pak church.

Rev. Robert wrote to me after his return to Pakistan about his experience at Camp Taconic: "'For I am not ashamed of the gospel of Christ: for it is the power of God unto salvation of every one'" (Rom. 1:16, KJV). Just as the furtherance of the gospel was

Rev. Alexander Robert baptizing a new convert

the nearest to the heart of Paul, so it is the top priority in my life. In the guidance of the Holy Spirit, I strongly believe that Jesus has called me and chosen me to implement His command to show Christ's love to the lost souls of Pakistan. I feel God has given me a visionary church that I can give my life in service to. So I have accepted the responsibility to shape the Church of the Nazarene in Pakistan to be a Spirit-empowered, holiness church and thus reveal God's divine will—His concern for the lost sheep of Pakistan."

Alexander immediately began to translate the church constitution from the Nazarene *Manual* and gospel tracts into Urdu. He was laying a solid foundation for the Church of the Nazarene in his country. Upon receiving these important documents from

Alexander, I contacted World Mission again and talked with Franklin Cook, director of the Eurasia Region. He arranged for David and me to meet with Louie Bustle and Hermann Gschwandtner in Nashville. From that meeting we were sent to visit Pakistan with Rev. Gschwandtner to assist with the opening of the country *behind the veil* as a mission field. In January 1995 we landed in Lahore and immediately began preaching to groups of people that Alexander had arranged.

8

Establishing the Church

Christians in Pakistan are virtually nonpersons. They are often discriminated against for significant middle-class job opportunities, and their children are almost excluded from education outside a mission school, which are few. Their housing is "primitive," largely in what the Western world would call *ghetto*. These ghettoes are marked by open sewers in the streets, polluted water, and assorted vermin. The living conditions are undesirable by most any world standard.

Hindus fare a little better than the Christian population. Only among the Christians, Hindus, and the 17 to 20 percent of declared nonreligious is the Church of the Nazarene permitted by the government to work. It is still a capital offense in Pakistan for a Muslim to convert to the Christian faith.

Yet, in this environment the church has grown rapidly.

"Amin, you are a very good car painter," the

stranger flattered. "Your work should make you wealthy. Don't just use it here in Pakistan."

Amin was proud of his work. The old car had sparkled to life with his expert painting skills. He knew he was one of the best car painters in Lahore, Pakistan. His excellent work had been praised by many satisfied customers.

The stranger came back to Amin, but this time with a specific offer. "Amin, I have contacts that could set you up in the Middle East, a much wealthier area. Your painting ability could make you rich." The "unknown" man then sketched a plan on how to establish a lucrative painting business.

Amin was captured by the plan to build such a profitable business. The idea sent Amin soliciting from his friends' financial investments. His excitement won the reluctant friends to invest much, and a few even promised to move with him to establish the business. Amin secured the necessary travel documents as soon as the venture capital was raised and delivered to the stranger.

Days and weeks went by. Waiting and waiting and more waiting. But the man with the too-good-to-be-true plan never returned. A devastated Amin tried to placate his friends. They were not forgiving. Time dragged on, and it became apparent that Amin and his fellow investors had been swindled.

Amin's friends demanded their investment be returned. He pleaded with them, but they gave him the ultimatum: "Pay up or we will meet you in court!"

Amin and his wife sold their house and paid off

the investors. Now destitute, the couple found shelter in a subhuman settlement that eliminated any hope of education for their children.

Living in this area was a member of the newly organized Church of the Nazarene mission started in 1995. This Nazarene met Amin, who soon shared his grief.

The Nazarene layman secured a place in the Nazarene Tailoring School for Amin's wife. Their two sons were enrolled in the Nazarene grammar school, and their 13-year-old daughter was admitted to St. Maria Nazarene High School.

> Prayer—*fervent, righteous prayer —is God's powerful answer to souls being saved.*

"Better than all this," the Pakistani pastor declared," Amin and his family have now experienced spiritual prosperity. They now know God's amazing grace. They have become vital Christians.

"What's the secret? Prayer," the pastor both asks and then answers. *Prayer*—fervent, righteous prayer —is God's powerful answer to souls being saved."

The five-year report at the 2000 Pakistan district assembly revealed just how significant the growth had been from that small group of believers. The increase of 501 new members in just one year brought the total district membership to 1,804 in 20 churches. With greater political turmoil, the growth continued with 10 new churches in 2001. A key fac-

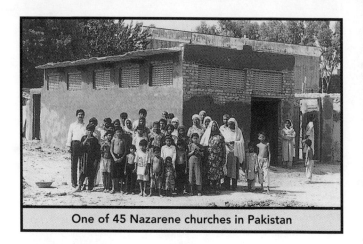

One of 45 Nazarene churches in Pakistan

tor in this growth has been the 8 teams showing the *JESUS* film in many new areas. And as opposition increased, the church also increased.

Rev. Robert was appointed district superintendent in 1998, and his makeshift office located in his own home was part of St. Maria School. In August of that year, World Mission provided funds to purchase an old 20' x 10' building from the owner, Mohammed Shafiq. An additional 15' x 15' space became available when Mohammed found a suitable house and moved.

Every Sunday the building was crowded beyond capacity. Through the nine-inch wall, Mohammed was treated to lively Christian music. "My friends make a mockery of me," Mohammed told Pastor Alexander. "They say, 'You, a fanatic Muslim, have started a Nazarene Christian Church right in your house.'" That helped the Muslim to hasten his departure.

In October the congregation celebrated its second birthday with 70 in attendance, made possible by the removal of the nine-inch wall. The church people visited, prayed, and preached, and soon the expanded structure was also inadequate.

When the congregation learned about Alabaster funds to assist in new church buildings, their request was honored with a grant of $4,950 to remodel and add to their present building.

"God impressed upon us," District Superintendent Robert said, "that we construct a new building on the unused property." They secured an architect but were discouraged by the estimated cost of $15,000 to erect a 35' x 75' building. Prayerful dis-

A Vacation Bible School in Lahore

cussion followed. Rev. Robert said to the church board, "I refuse to sanction such a project." Further discussion followed. Then the congregation agreed to start, proceed by faith, and build as offerings supplemented the grant.

In June 1999 the site work was completed, and the church members each signed a brick that became the foundation bricks the masons laid. Great rejoicing followed. Work could now progress unhindered because the Church of the Nazarene was officially registered in Pakistan.

District Superintendent Robert had wisely secured full registration of the church with the government three years earlier. "One month after the registration office sent the papers to the resident magistrates, a police van with five gun-carrying police came to St. Maria School. The highest ranking officer came to see the church that I was going to register," Alexander says.

Rev. Robert explained that it had not been erected yet. The officer guessed that the school was going to be demolished and the church built on the property. Alexander told him that he had registered the church or denomination, not a building site. So the police left.

A few days later Alexander received a message that the officer had written a negative report saying, "I have visited the site, and the church would be built within 70 feet of a Muslim mosque, and that will only create conflict."

After a fearful wait, Alexander secured an appointment with the resident magistrate of the area of Lahore. The meeting started poorly, as it was a great struggle to get the magistrate to understand the registration was from a denomination and for the entire country of Pakistan. When all seemed lost, the magistrate suddenly seemed to comprehend. The test was over; registration was fully granted.

During the construction the expenses increased beyond the architect's estimates. In the midst of the new shutdown, Hermann Gschwandtner from the Eurasia regional office visited. "This could be the largest Nazarene church building in South Asia," he said, astonished at what he observed. In spite of Hermann's joy, no further funds were available.

The Metro New York District became aware of the need and sent a special offering of $2,000. Rev. David Mall rejoiced over this special gift. While work was halted on the exterior, this gift from the States helped finish the inside, but without any seating. Everyone stood for worship.

When David died unexpectedly in December 2000, the Metro New York District and others contributed another $5,000 to help complete the church's exterior.

Dr. John Knight, general superintendent, led in the dedication of the first Nazarene church building in Lahore. "The name was changed to the David Mall Memorial Church in loving memory of this man of God," says Rev. Robert, "for his sacrificial service in starting the Church of the Nazarene in Pakistan."

The new church and adjacent old building are also the centers for a tailoring school, a computer-

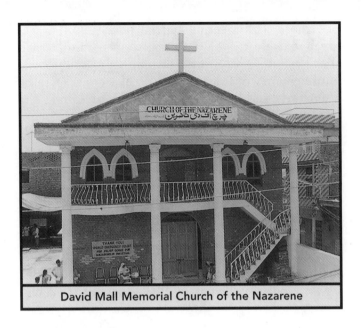
David Mall Memorial Church of the Nazarene

training program, and a secretarial school, as well as
housing the district offices. In December 2001
Robert Prescott of Nazarene Compassionate Ministries International donated a public address system,
and Alexander's son-in-law gave an organ. These
new additions have energized the Lahore choir.

In 2002 more than 100 students graduated
from the skill-center schools, helping prepare Nazarenes for garment factory and clerical positions.

Two new church buildings at Rawind and Pato-
ki have been constructed, and another building is
now desperately needed for a church with 70 members.

South Asia Nazarene Bible College has been established in both Karachi and Lahore with 20 students enrolled in pastoral training. Rev. Robert and Dr. Sohail Samuel head the five-person faculty at the two centers.

The district superintendent's outlandish vision of starting 50 churches in Pakistan and opening work in Afghanistan doesn't seem at all like idle speculation when we reflect on the opening seven years of the church. "This is but a small sample of what God is doing through the Church of the Nazarene in Pakistan. Difficult as it is for us, God is leading us to greater victories. We join hands with our fellow Nazarenes around the world to fulfill the call to save souls and sanctify believers."

> *The outlandish vision of starting 50 churches in Pakistan and opening work in Afghanistan doesn't seem at all like idle speculation when we reflect on the opening seven years of the church.*

Epilogue

Celebrating!

I had the privilege to chair the sixth assembly of the Pakistan District on January 26, 2003. What a celebration! What an uplifting expression of hope in Christ! The Pakistan pastors and leaders filled the assembly with the joy of anticipated help of the Holy Spirit in reaching nearly 1,000 new people and opening the doors for ministry in Afghanistan.

In this assembly the report indicated the following:

- 45 churches with a membership of 3,240
- a gain of 15 new churches and 910 members during the assembly year, 2002-03
- 30 ministers, several pastoring more than one church, are the result of an effective Nazarene Bible College

Most inspiring is that all of this hope in Christ is lived out in a climate of severe persecution and testings of various types—physical threats, ghetto-living conditions, discrimination in the job market, and reduced prospects for higher education.

Only 6 of the 45 congregations have adequate church buildings; many are still meeting on rooftops at night. The key churches are forced to hire armed guards to protect the worshipers. I trust that Alabaster funds will match Pakistani giving to foster growing congregations in building churches in the next few years.

Pakistani Nazarenes share with all Nazarenes in nearly full payment of their accepted World Evangelism Fund. Though small in dollars, it is given out of their "want."

I pray differently today for Pakistan because I fear for the lives of our pastors and people. But they shout with their very lives, "Onward! And next into Afghanistan!"

As David Mall and I stood on the dusty road of

Dr. Dallas Mucci *(right)* preaching with Rev. Alexander Robert interpreting at the Pakistan district assembly in 2003

Rev. Robert and Dr. Mucci *(front row center)* with all
Pakistani pastors at the district assembly in 2003

a ghetto in Lahore in 1995 and he dreamed a huge
dream of 10 Nazarene churches in 10 years, we both
laughed in weak faith. Now just look at what God
has done among the people called Nazarenes in the
land *behind the veil.*

Indeed, we have reason to celebrate!

Pronunciation Guide

The following information is provided to assist in pronouncing some unfamiliar words in this book. The suggested pronunciations, though not always precise, are close approximations of the way the terms are pronounced.

Amin	ah-MEEN
Aneel	ah-NEEL
Bashir Almas	ba-SHEER ahl-MAHS
Benghazi	behn-GAH-zee
Bhutto	BOO-toh
Bushra Hadayat	BUHSH-ruh huh-DAHT
Gschwandtner	gehsh-WAHND-ner
Islamabad	ihs-LAHM-uh-BAHD
Kabul	KAH-buhl
Karachi	kuh-RAH-chee
Lahore	luh-HOHR
Mouton	MOH-'uhn
Muammar Khaddafi	moo-AM-mahr kah-DAH-fee
Nayyar	NAY-yer
Noor, Rita	NOOR REE-tah
Patalano	pah-tah-LAH-noh
Patoki	poh-TOH-kee
Peshawar	puh-SHAH-wer
Punjab	puhn-JAHB
Rawind	RIE-wihnd
Shafiq	shah-FEEK
Sohail	soh-HAYL
Taconic	tuh-KAHN-ihk
Tamil	TAH-muhl
Urdu	ER-doo
Yasim Kasib	yah-SEEM KAH-suhb